IT'S A WONDERFUL LIFE

DAVID McLAUGHLAN

BARBOUR
PUBLISHING

Print ISBN 978-1-62416-244-2

eBook Editions:
Adobe Digital Edition (.epub) 978-1-62416-485-9
Kindle and MobiPocket Edition (.prc) 978-1-62416-484-2

Scripture quotations are taken from the King James Version of the Bible.

Published by Barbour Publishing, Inc., P.O. Box 719, Uhrichsville, Ohio 44683, www.barbourbooks.com

Our mission is to publish and distribute inspirational products offering exceptional value and biblical encouragement to the masses.

Member of the
Evangelical Christian
Publishers Association

Printed in the United States of America.

Contents

Introduction

Yes, it is a wonderful life.

Here's a fun, nostalgic, encouraging month's worth of reading for the busy holiday season!

This brand-new Christmas devotional includes thirty-one brief readings based on Christmas classics—stories, books, movies, poems, and songs. Each entry draws a spiritual point from a classic story, whether sacred or secular, and is accompanied by relevant quotations, scriptures, and prayers.

Entries range from the namesake 1946 film starring Jimmie Stewart, to Charles Dickens' *A Christmas Carol,* to the 1965 television favorite *A Charlie Brown Christmas*—and end with the actual account of Jesus' birth from Luke 2.

It really *is* a wonderful life—because of Christmas!

1.
It's a Wonderful Life

George Bailey is usually seen as the archetypal good guy, but, on closer inspection, he is rather like one of those cartoon characters with a devil on one shoulder and an angel on the other.

Growing up in Bedford Falls, he learns Christian charity from his father and sees selfish evil in "Old Man" Potter. He follows his dad's good example, stands up for the little guy, and always puts others before himself, but the devil on his shoulder keeps tempting him with dreams of a better life in foreign places.

Eventually, when it seems none of those dreams will ever come true, that voice of failure and despair takes George to a bridge and convinces him to end it all. That's when Clarence, an angel in training, shows him the difference his life made to his hometown. If he'd gone travelling, as the devil kept telling him to, Mr. Potter would have ruined Bedford

Falls and countless lives.

Realizing his sacrifices have been worthwhile, George asks God for a second chance. All the ingredients for a happy ending are in place—except one. It's Christmas Eve and he's about to lose his home!

Hearing that George and his family are in trouble, the townspeople gather all the cash they can spare and present it to him. For the first time George Bailey allows himself to be helped. For the moviegoers this is the point where the happy tears well up.

"Love thy neighbour." It's straightforward enough. "Give, and it shall be given unto you." We've heard it so often. But we have to allow our neighbor to love us as well. That's why the movie isn't complete until George Bailey, the man who spent his life helping others, is helped. When we finally understand that loving each other is why we are here, and we allow them to love us in return, that's when it truly does become a wonderful life!

Those Little Extras

- Philip Van Doren Stern wrote *It's a Wonderful Life* in 1939—after it came to him in a dream.

- The story was originally called "The Greatest Gift."

- The 1946 movie by Frank Capra was nominated for five Oscars. Amazingly, it won none!

- James Stewart played George Bailey; Donna Reed played his ever-supportive wife; Henry Travers was Clarence, the angel in training; and Lionel Barrymore played George Bailey's nemesis, Henry F. Potter.

To the Gift Giver

Lord, Your plans are bigger and better than my dreams. Help me see that. And help me see that my joy in doing Your work is not complete unless I can receive Your love as well as give it. May I share that joy with and through those who have much and those with nothing more than a smile to offer. Let me allow them what You allow me—the blessing of being able to give.

❄

From the Gift Giver

Hitherto have ye asked nothing in my name: ask, and ye shall receive, that your joy may be full.

JOHN 16:24

Other *Wonderful* Thoughts. . .

For it is in giving that we receive.

FRANCIS OF ASSISI,
FOUNDER OF THE FRANCISCAN ORDER
(1181–1226)

When you give of yourself,
you receive more than you give.

ANTOINE DE SAINT-EXUPERY,
FRENCH POET AND AVIATOR
(1900–1944)

All of us, at certain moments of our lives, need to take
advice and receive help from other people.

ALEXIS CARREL,
FRENCH NOBEL PRIZE WINNER
(1873–1944)

All who call on God in true faith, earnestly from the
heart, will certainly be heard, and will receive what
they have asked and desired.

MARTIN LUTHER,
LEADING FIGURE IN THE PROTESTANT
REFORMATION (1483–1546)

2.
A Christmas Carol

We usually think of *A Christmas Carol* as the tale of Ebenezer Scrooge. In him we see what happens to a man who surrounds himself with treasures on earth while completely neglecting the treasures of heaven. But while Scrooge is the more dramatic character, we should not forget another player in the story—Scrooge's nephew!

Every year Fred visits his uncle and invites him to Christmas dinner. He knows he will be rebuffed but, because it is the decent thing to do, he tries. He admits that Uncle Scrooge is "not so pleasant as he might be. However, his offences carry their own punishment, and I have nothing to say against him."

So Fred was a nice guy, and forgiving, and possibly fond of the old curmudgeon, but did he make a difference? The Spirit of Christmas Past showed Scrooge he hadn't always been that way.

Christmas Present showed him what he was depriving himself and others of. Christmas Future showed him where his chosen path would inevitably end. They turned him around.

Ahh, but nephew Fred, in his lack of condemnation, gave Scrooge a place to turn *to*; a family among whom a lonely old miser might blossom into a human being again.

Few of us will ever be as cut off from humanity as Scrooge was, and fewer still will have the experiences he had—but every single one of us, at some time or another, will have the chance to let an insult slide past while keeping out that hand of friendship.

Young Fred might not have forgiven his Uncle Scrooge seventy times seven times, as the Bible says, but he would have! If we can do what Fred did for Scrooge, what God does for us, we might also see lives transformed. Then we could happily join the angels in heaven in singing a Christmas carol, no matter what time of year it was!

Those Little Extras

- Charles Dickens based the story on hard times suffered by his father. It was an instant success!

- Ebenezer Scrooge has been portrayed on the screen by Jim Carrey, Michael Cain, Albert Finney, Kelsey Grammer, Tom Hanks, and many others.

- *A Christmas Carol* is credited with restoring Christmas as a celebratory holiday after a long period of sober remembrance.

- The novella was published in 1843 and has been in print ever since.

To the Gift Giver

Lord, broken people will reject us and our love,
but if we give in or react in hurt, then hate wins.
The world rejected You on the cross—but You
kept on loving it! Walk close beside us in difficult
times so that through Your love, patience, and
understanding, we might help heal others and
turn lives around.

❄

From the Gift Giver

*Then came Peter to him, and said, Lord, how oft shall
my brother sin against me, and I forgive him? till
seven times? Jesus saith unto him,
I say not unto thee, Until seven times: but,
Until seventy times seven.*

MATTHEW 18:21–22

Other Wonderful Thoughts. . .

If you judge people, you have no time to love them.

MOTHER TERESA,
FOUNDER OF THE MISSIONARIES OF CHARITY
(1910–1997)

*To be a Christian means to forgive the inexcusable
because God has forgiven the inexcusable in you.*

C. S. LEWIS,
ACADEMIC AND NOVELIST
(1898–1963)

*Forgiveness is not an occasional act,
it is a constant attitude.*

MARTIN LUTHER KING, JR.,
MINISTER AND CIVIL RIGHTS ACTIVIST
(1929–1968)

*To love means loving the unlovable.
To forgive means pardoning the unpardonable.
Faith means believing the unbelievable. Hope means
hoping when everything seems hopeless.*

G. K. CHESTERTON,
NOVELIST AND CHRISTIAN APOLOGIST
(1874–1936)

3.
"The Gift of the Magi"

Jim and Della face a classic December dilemma—what to get the one you love for Christmas. To complicate matters, they have very little money. Della has been saving her pennies, but pennies can't express the love she has for her husband. To do that she has to do more than just haggle with storekeepers over the cost of comestibles; she needs to venture into the realm of sacrifice.

The young couple each has one prized possession. Jim has his grandfather's watch, which he is sure would make Solomon look askance at his fabled treasure. Della has her long, shining tresses, hair she knows even the Queen of Sheba would envy.

So Della sells her hair, despite the fear that Jim might not find her attractive afterward, for the cash to buy a chain for his grandfather's watch. The gift she gives him is, literally, of herself.

Jim is, of course, stunned. When he recovers, he immediately assures her she will always be beautiful to him. Then he laughs! You see, he has sold his heirloom, his connection to his family's past, his grandfather's watch—to buy combs for Della's hair!

Both gifts are useless, but precious beyond money! Both Jim and Della were left knowing, beyond any doubt, that they were the most important thing in the other one's life.

The Wise Men, the Magi, didn't give gifts that reflected their bank balances. Through their gifts they tried to reflect the value of the One they were giving to.

So, how do those of us who aren't foreign potentates do that? We do what Della did, we do what Jim did, we do what Jesus did at Calvary. . . we give of ourselves.

Of course, gadgets and books and games will always be fun, but if you want to give wisely, like a Magi, then give of yourself.

Those Little Extras

- "The Gift of the Magi" was written by O. Henry, whose real name was William Sydney Porter.

- It appeared in the collection *The Four Million*. The title was an affectionate nod to the citizens of New York, every one of whom, he felt, had a story to tell.

- Published in 1906, it was filmed three years later as *The Sacrifice*.

- The story has been retold many times, notably by Mickey Mouse and the Sesame Street gang.

To the Gift Giver

Lord, You didn't show Your love by sending us a gift voucher; You became human and died for us. It was the most personal gift possible. There's a time for store-bought presents and a time for something a little more personal. Don't let fear or embarrassment keep us from giving in the best way—from the heart, to our brothers and sisters.

❄

From the Gift Giver

And when they were come into the house, they saw the young child with Mary his mother, and fell down, and worshipped him: and when they had opened their treasures, they presented unto him gifts; gold, and frankincense and myrrh.

MATTHEW 2:11

Other Wonderful Thoughts. . .

*You can give without loving,
but you cannot love without giving.*

AMY WILSON CARMICHAEL,
IRISH MISSIONARY TO INDIA
(1867–1951)

One must be poor to know the luxury of giving.

GEORGE ELIOT (MARY ANNE EVANS),
ENGLISH NOVELIST
(1819–1880)

*No person was ever honored for what he received.
Honor has been the reward for what he gave.*

CALVIN COOLIDGE,
THIRTIETH PRESIDENT OF THE UNITED STATES
(1872–1933)

*Give what you have. To someone, it may
be better than you dare to think.*

HENRY WADSWORTH LONGFELLOW,
AMERICAN POET
(1807–1882)

4.
"Twas the Night Before Christmas"

Tradition has it that every year in the General Theological College, in New York City, students hang a wreath around a painting of Clement Clarke Moore.

If Moore, who died in 1863, could have foreseen this, he might have thought it was because he donated the land the college was built upon. Or he might have thought it was in tribute to some of his scholarly works. He would never have imagined it was because of a poem he wrote for his children!

That poem was "A Visit from Saint Nicholas," also known as "'Twas the Night Before Christmas"! It would have been an essential part of Christmas for the students hanging the wreath—and for children across the world in the generations between Clarke and the present!

This was the verse that, for the first time, presented Saint Nicholas as the Santa Claus we recognize today. Here we have the reindeers and their names, the flying sleigh, and Santa coming down a chimney.

Would he have been surprised at being remembered for such a thing? Probably! Should he have been surprised?

All too often great works are superseded in the popular imagination by simple acts of humanity. Newton is remembered for an apple falling on his head. Washington may be most remembered for his encounter with a cherry tree.

Christ was the Word through which the universe was created, but we remember Him most fondly for being born in a stable, for calling the children to Him, for healing and forgiving.

We make a mistake when we think life is about material achievement. We make our biggest impact on the world when we offer simple kindness, when we touch hearts, when we make a child smile. And the author of "'Twas the Night Before Christmas," possibly to his very great surprise, has made thousands of children smile!

Those Little Extras

- "A Visit from Saint Nicholas" is generally thought to be the best-known piece of American poetry ever written.

- Santa Claus is never mentioned in the poem.

- Moore is said to have based his description on a local Dutch handyman.

- The "jolly old elf" actually arrives on Christmas Eve rather than Christmas Day.

To the Gift Giver

Dear Lord, in this world it often seems like the only way to succeed is to "get ahead," to own more, to achieve more. But that driving urge all too often separates us from You. Help us remember that the world's victories are not victories You would recognize. Keep us secure in the little things, Lord, the kind word, the outstretched hand, the forgiving attitude. In short, keep us where You are.

❄

From the Gift Giver

But Jesus called them unto him, and said, Suffer little children to come unto me, and forbid them not: for of such is the kingdom of God.

LUKE 18:16

Other Wonderful Thoughts. . .

*I don't really care how I am remembered as
long as I bring happiness and joy to people.*

EDDIE ALBERT, ACTOR
(1906–2005)

*I am certain that after the dust of centuries has
passed over our cities, we, too, will be remembered, not
for victories or defeats in battle or in politics, but for our
contribution to the human spirit.*

JOHN FITZGERALD KENNEDY,
THIRTY-FIFTH PRESIDENT OF THE UNITED STATES
(1917–1963)

To live in hearts we leave behind is not to die.

THOMAS CAMPBELL, SCOTTISH POET
(1777–1844)

*One hundred years from now it will not matter
what kind of car I drove, what kind of house
I lived in, or how much money I had in the bank.
But the world may be a better place because
I made a difference in a child's life.*

FOREST E. WITCRAFT,
BOY SCOUT ADMINISTRATOR
(1894–1967)

5.
"Good King Wenceslas"

Good King Wenceslas wasn't a king—but he *was* good!

A tenth-century duke of Bohemia, he became known for his piety and charitable works. After his death, at age twenty-eight, the Holy Roman Emperor proclaimed him a "righteous king."

His reign was notable for the example he set and the example he followed. He set the example of a father looking after his children, especially those in need. In visiting the poor, the sick, and the prisoners, Wenceslas followed the example of his Lord, Jesus Christ.

As Wenceslas followed Jesus, so his page boy, Podevin, followed Wenceslas. The carol has them setting out on a midwinter mission of mercy. As they carry supplies through the snow Podevin's strength deserts him. Wenceslas tells him to walk in his king's footsteps. This makes the going easier, but there is also a life-giving warmth in those foot-prints that revives the boy, enabling him to keep going.

A fanciful story? Perhaps, but Wenceslas' real life made it believable.

It was a hard time, and the world isn't kind to such goodness in the best of times. He was killed by his pagan brother, whose nickname was "the cruel" and whose given name is probably best for-gotten. But Wenceslas's example lives on, in the Christmas carol and in his sainthood, because he followed the best example there is.

According to the carol, Wenceslas tells Podevin, "Mark my footsteps, my good page. Tread thou in them boldly."

Jesus calls us to follow Him as Wenceslas called Podevin. The best way we can possibly do that is by treading boldly in His footsteps, draw-ing strength from His example, and moving for-ward together, like page and monarch, like the Christmas Spirit and Christmas, like beloved and lover, like saved and Savior, like humble subject and the original Righteous King!

Those Little Extras

- Wenceslas's mother may have held pagan beliefs, but he was raised by his Christian grandmother.

- John Mason Neale, who translated many hymns we sing today, wrote "Good King Wenceslas."

- The tune is based on an old folk song welcoming spring.

- "Good King Wenceslas" was first published in 1853.

To the Gift Giver

Lord, it's not as if we don't know what we should do. But we live in a world of excuses, under the influence of a great deceiver. Give us the heart to follow in Your footsteps regardless of what others think of us in this life, because in Your footsteps lie the sustaining warmth of real life!

❄

From the Gift Giver

*And as Jesus passed forth from thence, he saw a man,
named Matthew, sitting at the receipt of custom:
and he saith unto him, Follow me.
And he arose, and followed him.*

MATTHEW 9:9

Other Wonderful Thoughts. . .

Whatsoever one would understand what he hears must hasten to put into practice what he has heard.

GREGORY THE GREAT, "THE FATHER OF
CHRISTIAN WORSHIP" (C. 540–604)

Let this be thy whole endeavor, this thy prayer, this thy desire—that thou mayest be stripped of all selfishness, and with entire simplicity follow Jesus only.

THOMAS À KEMPIS, AUTHOR OF
THE IMITATION OF CHRIST (1380–1471)

*In the footsteps of my Savior I would walk each day,
Following ever where they'd lead me,
Close to Him to stay.*

AUTHOR UNKNOWN

*Nothing is really lost by a life of sacrifice;
everything is lost by failure to obey God's call.*

HENRY P. LIDDON, ENGLISH THEOLOGIAN
(1829–1890)

6.
Frosty the Snowman

Frosty the Snowman started life as a song, a successor of sorts to "Rudolph the Red-Nosed Reindeer." It soon became a much-loved part of the Christmas tradition, so it must have seemed like a good idea to expand it into an animated story for a new generation of children.

Jimmy Durante takes the role of the narrator, telling how some schoolchildren, on the last day of school, build a snowman then bring it to life with a magician's hat. But from the start Durante makes it plain that the real magic is in the quality of the snow, because it is Christmas snow!

Of course, snowmen don't last forever, and Frosty's friend Karen can't abide the thought of him melting, so she decides to take him to the North Pole where he can live forever. They stow away in a refrigerated boxcar, which is a great way for a snowman to travel, but not so healthy for little girls!

Soon Frosty has to abandon his journey and get Karen somewhere warm before it's too late for her. He finds her a cozy greenhouse where Christmas poinsettias are growing. Unfortunately, it's so warm it melts Frosty!

But Santa comes to the rescue. He tells Karen that because Frosty was made from Christmas snow he can be born again, just as Christmas is born again every year. Frosty returns and lives to this day with Santa at the North Pole, while Karen is returned safely home.

It's a fun song, and an entertaining animation, but themes of Christmas are still there; birth, death, and rebirth, the friends save each other through their love, and, of course, there is sacrifice.

Love and sacrifice always warm our hearts, even at the North Pole. And why? Because they are what God is all about—and Frosty, and Karen, and, hopefully, everyone who loves Christmas and charming Christmas tales like this!

Those Little Extras

- The song "Frosty the Snowman" was written by Walter Rollins and Steve Nelson.

- The song was recorded by Gene Autry in 1950 and reached number seven on the US pop charts.

- The television special was first aired on December 7, 1969.

- Comedian Jackie Vernon played Frosty.

To the Gift Giver

Sometimes, Lord, You must think us deliberately blind. This creation of Yours is all about new life. Seasons come and go—and new seasons come. Plants die back and grow again in spring. Each new generation renews a family. The sun always rises. Why would we doubt that after we fall we will also rise?

❄

From the Gift Giver

And the angel answered and said unto the women, Fear not ye: for I know that ye seek Jesus, which was crucified. He is not here: for he is risen, as he said. Come, see the place where the Lord lay.

MATTHEW 28:5–6

Other Wonderful Thoughts. . .

My sun sets to rise again.

Robert Browning, English poet
and playwright (1812–1889)

*It boggles my mind that someone can see life
breathed into a baby, watch the grass die then come
back to life again, see leaves fall and watch the
rebirth of a tree, or gaze on any of the majestic
splendor that is this earth and not be overpowered
by the presence of an Almighty God.*

Bill McCartney, founder of Promise Keepers
(born 1940)

*Self-sacrifice is the real miracle out of which
all the reported miracles grow.*

Ralph Waldo Emerson, essayist and poet
(1803–1882)

*Behold, I do not give lectures or a little charity,
When I give, I give myself.*

Walt Whitman, essayist and poet (1819–1892)

7.
A Charlie Brown Christmas

As far back as 1965 Charlie Brown was worried that Christmas had become too commercial!

In *A Charlie Brown Christmas* our hero just can't get into the spirit of the season. So Lucy invites him to direct their school play.

Unwittingly, Charlie Brown himself hints at what's missing when he shouts to the cast, "One of the first things to ensure a good performance is strict attention to the director!" Those of us who trust the Holy Spirit as our director are never far away from a "good performance."

In his normal intuitive manner Charlie Brown stumbles across the secret. Looking for a Christmas tree, he ignores the fancy, illuminated, aluminum specimens and buys a needle-shedding, stunted little fir tree. He's on the right track. At Christmastime, perhaps more than any other time of the year, the faithful among us ought to look out for the weak, the poor, the dispossessed.

As usual, though, Charlie Brown goes about caring for the little tree in the wrong way. He takes a decoration from Snoopy's prize-winning decorated dog house and tries to make his tree special in a worldly way. But the single shiny globe bends the poor tree right over.

It's Linus who shows us what is really needed. He makes the tree feel special by wrapping his blanket around it—the blanket he is never usually separated from. Linus gives of himself—and the transformation is miraculous!

Christmas is more commercial now than it was when *A Charlie Brown Christmas* was first broadcast, and it will probably become even more so in the years ahead. But so long as one person reaches out to someone (or something) in need, as Charlie Brown did, so long as someone gives a gift purely from love, as Linus did, then the "director" of Christmas will be right there beside us—applauding!

Those Little Extras

- *A Charlie Brown Christmas* was the first prime-time animation based on the Peanuts comic strip.

- The first airing was sponsored by Coca-Cola.

- It won an Emmy and a Peabody Award.

- Peter Robbins was the voice of Charlie Brown (Pigpen, too).

To the Gift Giver

Dear Lord, those of us who have been down know the wonder of a hand up; those who have grieved wouldn't swap a comforting hug for any amount of money; those who had no one left to turn to know that only You could have sent the stranger to our aid. In doing the same for others we will be content, knowing we have You either beside us or in front of us.

❄

From the Gift Giver

Then shall he answer them, saying, Verily I say unto you, Inasmuch as ye did it not to one of the least of these, ye did it not to me.

MATTHEW 25:45

Other Wonderful Thoughts. . .

*"I never thought it was such a bad little tree.
It's not bad at all, really. Maybe it just needs a little love."*

CHARLES SCHULZ, CARTOONIST (1922–2000),
SPOKEN BY LINUS VAN PELT IN
A CHARLIE BROWN CHRISTMAS

*The best of all gifts around any Christmas tree:
the presence of a happy family all wrapped up in each other.*

BURTON HILLIS (WILLIAM E. VAUGHAN),
COLUMNIST AND AUTHOR (1915–1977)

*The perfect Christmas tree?
All Christmas trees are perfect!*

CHARLES N. BARNARD, TRAVEL WRITER
AND MAGAZINE EDITOR (BORN 1924)

*The Earth reminded us of a Christmas tree ornament
hanging in the blackness of space. As we got farther
and farther away it diminished in size. Finally it
shrank to the size of a marble, the most beautiful
marble you can imagine.*

JAMES IRWIN, APOLLO 15 ASTRONAUT
(1930–1991)

8.
How the Grinch Stole Christmas!

The Grinch is an outsider! Dr. Seuss didn't explain why, but he didn't have to. Every society has them, most of us have felt like one at some point, and in the mid-1960s the "outsiders" were our hippy/counter-culture/drug-taking teenagers.

Slouching against a wall with a sneer on his face and chewing on a toothpick, the Grinch could have been the archetypal teenage rebel.

With a very Dr. Seuss twist, however, the establishment, the residents of Whoville, are more psychedelic, more "out there" than the Grinch!

But still, he is the outsider. In the 1966 television special, in a piece of inspired casting, Boris Karloff—who'd previously portrayed Frankenstein's monster—became the narrator and the voice of the Grinch.

Anticipating the fun the Whos will have at Christmas, the Grinch disguises himself as Santa and sneaks into Whoville. He steals every single Christmas-related item he can find, even down to the leaves of the poinsettias.

Preparing to throw all his Christmas booty off a mountain, he decides to wait and enjoy the misery when the Whos wake up on an un-Christmassy Christmas morning. To his amazement Christmas (looking very like the Star of Bethlehem) still comes to the village, and the Whos start celebrating!

When it occurs to the Grinch that true Christmas isn't store bought, he decides he wants some of that. He gives the presents back and joins the welcoming Whos for Christmas dinner!

Lack of acceptance, lack of understanding, fear, a natural desire to rebel against "the establishment"; all of these things mean there will be outsiders as long as there is such a thing as society, but Christian love is the cure for all that. The outsiders, be they our own children, the dispossessed, or green creatures prone to talking in rhyme, won't ever have to steal Christmas, if we give it to them as a gift first!

Those Little Extras

- Written in rhyming verse, *How The Grinch Stole Christmas!* was first published in 1957.

- The TV special was first aired in 1966.

- Boris Karloff played the role of the Grinch late in his career.

- The mountain the Grinch lives on is called Mount Crumpit.

- One critic rated its first showing as "passable," but it has gone on to become a television classic.

To the Gift Giver

In our fear and self-importance, Lord, we judge people and shut them out, either actively or through our indifference. We need to remember that You are indifferent to none of Your children, and no one is shut out when it comes to Your love. Give us the courage to reach out, beyond our own strengths and abilities, and bring some "lost sheep" home.

❄

From the Gift Giver

The Son of man came eating and drinking, and they say, Behold a man gluttonous, and a winebibber, a friend of publicans and sinners. But wisdom is justified of her children.

MATTHEW 11:19

Other Wonderful Thoughts. . .

In God's family, there are no outsiders, no enemies.

DESMOND TUTU, ANGLICAN BISHOP AND OPPONENT
OF APARTHEID (BORN 1931)

*He whom God has touched will always be a
being apart: he is, whatever he may do, a stranger
among men: he is marked by a sign.*

ERNEST RENAN, FRENCH LINGUIST AND WRITER
(1823–1892)

*Stranger, if you passing meet me and desire
to speak to me, why should you not speak to me?
And why should I not speak to you?*

WALT WHITMAN, ESSAYIST AND POET (1819–1892)

A stranger is just a friend I haven't met yet.

WILL ROGERS, ENTERTAINER (1879–1935)

9.
Rudolph the Red-Nosed Reindeer

The 1964 TV adaptation of *Rudolph the Red-Nosed Reindeer* is a tale of misfits. There's Rudolph, born with a nose that glows in the dark; Hermey, the toy-maker elf who really wants to be a dentist; Yukon Cornelius, the dogsled driver who usually ends up pulling the sled while his huskies sit on it; and the Bumble (abominable) Snow Monster.

Tired of being teased, Rudolph runs away, and the Bumble decides to have him for lunch! If it can't have him, it'll have his family! Rudolph defends his family with his new antlers, Yukon Cornelius drops an avalanche on it, and Hermey removes all its scary teeth.

Back at Christmas Town, Santa comes to the conclusion that even misfits have a place. Yukon Cornelius brings a tame Bumble into town, and they discover it's tall enough to put the star on the Christmas tree. Hermey begins looking after everyone's teeth. And Rudolph?

A snowstorm surrounds the town, and a despairing Santa concludes he can't fly the sleigh if he can't see where he's going. Then Rudolph's nose starts to glow, and, because of his guiding light, the children of the world get their Christmas gifts!

Santa isn't the only one with a soft spot for misfits. Jesus seemed to spend most of His time with them. But, then, He knew a secret. Just as all the odd characters in the Christmas special had a vital role to play in the story, so do those of us who might think ourselves odd in real life. The point is God doesn't make misfits. We all have an important role to play, and we fit in somewhere.

We may have to navigate the "snowstorm" of life for a while, but, with God as our guiding light instead of Rudolph, we'll get there and find the place, the profession, or the person He made us for!

Those Little Extras

- The song "Rudolph the Red-Nosed Reindeer" was recorded in 1949.

- It gave Gene Autry a number-one hit.

- Burl Ives is the snowman narrator in the TV special.

- Romeo Muller, who also wrote material for Jack Benny, wrote the story for the TV special.

To the Gift Giver

Merciful Lord, "Legion" was possessed and a danger to all around. Yet, you took this "misfit" and used him to your glory. I offer my faults, my undiscovered talents, my awkwardness, my passions, my childish devotion, all that I am, to You, in the assurance that, if it be Your will, glorious things will come of them.

❈

From the Gift Giver

And he departed, and began to publish in Decapolis how great things Jesus had done for him: and all men did marvel.

MARK 5:20

Other *Wonderful Thoughts*. . .

Hide not your talents, they for use were made.
What's a sundial in the shade?

BENJAMIN FRANKLIN, AMERICAN FOUNDING
FATHER AND POLYMATH (1706–1790)

And I said to the man who stood at the gate of the year:
"Give me a light that I may tread safely into the
unknown." And he replied: "Go into the darkness and
put your hand into the Hand of God. That shall be to you
better than light and safer than a known way."

MINNIE LOUISE HASKINS, BRITISH ACADEMIC AND POET
(1875–1957)

Nature has concealed at the bottom of our minds talents
and abilities of which we are not aware.

FRANÇOIS DE LA ROCHEFOUCAULD, FRENCH PRINCE
AND AUTHOR (1613–1680)

A great deal of talent is lost to the
world for want of a little courage.

SYDNEY SMITH, ENGLISH WRITER AND CLERGYMAN
(1771–1845)

10.
"The Fir-Tree"

At first reading the story "The Fir-Tree" seems like a lesson on seizing the day.

As a sapling, the fir tree pays no heed to the passing children; sunshine is disregarded; the squirrels who run along his branches are ignored; he barely sees the sparkling snow in wintertime.

He just wants to be taller.

Taller neighbors are cut down for ships masts, and the Fir Tree envies them their adventures.

Other trees are cut for Christmas, and he envies them their decorations. This time he gets his wish, and he is taken to a home and dressed beautifully. Everyone pays attention to him—but he is too nervous to enjoy it. He promises himself he will enjoy it tomorrow. But when tomorrow comes the tree is discarded.

At each step of the story the fir tree is surrounded by the blessings of God, but he is too busy longing for what he doesn't have to appreciate all he has been given.

Still, there is another part of the story. A small but important part. In his short time as a beautiful Christmas tree, he hears the story of Humpty Dumpty.

In the version we know today Humpty Dumpty has a great fall and can't be put together again. In Hans Christian Andersen's version Humpty Dumpty rises again—and is married! It was the only story the fir tree ever heard.

Hans Christian Andersen was the master storyteller. Choosing to put one story, and only one, within his tale of "The Fir-Tree," he could not have chosen better than a story of redemption.

As fallen beings, we are like Humpty Dumpty, but let's not be like the fir tree. Let's enjoy the blessings of creation every day, until we fall, rise again, and heaven and earth are married in the greatest "happily ever after" ever!

Those Little Extras

- Hans Christian Andersen published "The Fir-Tree" in 1844.

- It was noted as being unusually downbeat for the normally happy storyteller.

- It was included in the book, *New Fairy Tales*, first volume, second collection.

- Wilhelm Grimm (of the Brothers Grimm) heard Andersen read "The Fir-Tree" at Count Bismarck-Bohlen's Christmas party and reportedly liked it.

To the Gift Giver

Lord, we look for miracles while You try to tell us it is all a miracle. The moments we spend wishing we were elsewhere—miracles! The very thoughts we think while being unappreciative—miracles. The rain we resent—a miracle. The face we wish was prettier or more handsome—a wonderful miracle. If we had eyes to truly see Your work, every breath would be a gasp of awe!

❄

From the Gift Giver

In the beginning was the Word, and the Word was with God, and the Word was God. The same was in the beginning with God. All things were made by him; and without him was not any thing made that was made.

JOHN 1:1–3

Other Wonderful Thoughts. . .

God's purpose in redemption is glory, glory, glory!

WATCHMAN NEE (NI SHU-ZU),
CHINESE EVANGELIST (1903–1972)

Hail, thou ever-blessed morn!
Hail, redemption's happy dawn!

EDWARD CASWALL, ENGLISH CLERGYMAN AND
HYMN WRITER (1814–1878)

Every second is of infinite value.

JOHANN WOLFGANG VON GOETHE,
GERMAN WRITER AND POLITICIAN (1749–1832)

Know the true value of time;
snatch, seize, and enjoy every moment of it.
LORD CHESTERFIELD, ENGLISH EARL (1694–1773)

11

The Story of the Other Wise Man

Anyone who knows the Christmas story will have heard of Caspar, Melchior, and Balthazar, the Magi, the Three Kings, the Three Wise Men. But Henry Van Dyke tells us of a fourth Wise Man— Artaban!

Setting out in a hurry to meet the other Magi, he stops to help a man dying in the desert, and he misses the caravan. Thereafter he is always just one step behind. He arrives in Bethlehem too late for find the baby Jesus. But he saves another child from King Herod's rampaging soldiers. He travels to Egypt and finds, not his King, but countless other people to help with his healing skills.

Thirty-three years after he began his quest, he gets to Jerusalem in time for the crucifixion but misses seeing his Lord because he is buying a young woman her freedom with the last of the gifts he brought for the Christ.

As the earth shakes, as Jesus dies, a loose slate falls from a roof and strikes Artaban a mortal blow. He faces death convinced he has failed in what he set out to do—find the King of heaven.

As he leaves this life a quiet voice assures Artaban that he has seen Jesus many times, and Jesus has seen him.

Artaban's story is our story. Twenty centuries separate us from the earthly life of Jesus the man. Search as we will, we are unlikely to meet him in the way Artaban hoped to, but, in the words of the Lord himself, "Inasmuch as ye have done it unto one of the least of these my brethren, ye have done it unto me" (Matthew 25:40).

In comforting the sick, protecting the weak, and caring for the prisoner, Artaban was constantly with Jesus. If you or I would be the Other Wise Man (or Wise Woman), then we should do the same.

Those Little Extras

- *The Story of the Other Wise Man* was first published in 1895.

- A TV adaptation by Hallmark Hall of Fame was aired in 1953.

- In the year 2000 an opera based on the story was first performed.

- *Harper's New Monthly Magazine* described the story as, "So beautiful and so true to what is best in our natures, and so full of the Christmas spirit."

To the Gift Giver

The Wise Men had a unique opportunity, and they took it. Their journey might have been a long one; it might have been expensive, dangerous even; but they took it. Thanks to Your sacrifice, Lord, we have a better opportunity. You walk with us and You place Yourself in front of us day by day. May we be wise enough to see You.

✳

From the Gift Giver

Now when Jesus was born in Bethlehem of Judaea in the days of Herod the king, behold, there came wise men from the east to Jerusalem, saying, Where is he that is born King of the Jews? For we have seen his star in the east, and are come to worship him.

MATTHEW 2:1–2

Other Wonderful Thoughts. . .

*I cannot imagine how religious persons can live
satisfied without the practice of the presence of God.
For my part I keep myself retired with Him in the
depth of centre of my soul as much as I can;
and while I am so with Him I fear nothing; but the
least turning from Him is insupportable.*

BROTHER LAWRENCE, FRENCH LAY BROTHER
(C. 1614–1691)

*The most precious thing about Jesus is the fact that He is
not the great discourager, but the great encourager.*

WILLIAM BARCLAY, SCOTTISH AUTHOR
AND THEOLOGIAN (1907–1978)

*There is no one so lost that
Jesus cannot find him and save him.*

ANDREW MURRAY, SOUTH AFRICAN PREACHER
(1828–1917)

*In your teaching, let not your end be
to seek and find out curiosities and subtleties,
but to find and meet with Christ.*

THOMAS TAYLOR, ENGLISH PURITAN (1576–1633)

12.
"I Heard the Bells on Christmas Day"

There are few things more damaging to faith than despair, but that same despair can often produce exquisite outpourings of faith.

Henry Wadsworth Longfellow knew about despair. America was in the midst of civil war; his wife had died, leaving him to raise their two sons. One of those sons had enlisted.

Then, as December 1863 moved toward Christmas, he found himself nursing that son after he had been shot.

How many would have sung God's praises at that moment?

Wordsworth turned to poetry, and the first few stanzas of his poem, "Christmas Bells," seem surprisingly upbeat. He wrote of an "unbroken song," centuries of church bells proclaiming a message of peace on earth and goodwill to all men. Then the cannons of the war explode into his verse, and all that hope seems to have been for nothing.

Hate, it seemed, was the dominant force on earth. And, not knowing that his son would recover, not knowing if the war would ever end, hate's dominion must have seemed a very real possibility.

But Wordsworth's faith was stronger than his fear. He wrote on, laying down in ink the words he heard from the bells:

> *God is not dead; nor doth He sleep!*
> *The Wrong shall fail, The Right prevail,*
> *With peace on earth, good-will to men!*

There have been very few years where a war hasn't raged somewhere in the world. But there have been *no* years where peace and goodwill have not also been in the world. And a greater peace is coming.

There are still battles to be fought, in the world and in our lives, and each one is another closer to the ultimate victory. So, when the struggle seems too much, when despair is all around, sing along with Wordsworth's Christmas bells, "God is not dead; nor doth He sleep!" And there will be peace on earth!

Those Little Extras

- "I Heard the Bells on Christmas Day" is a Christmas carol based on the 1863 poem "Christmas Bells."

- Longfellow's son recovered and spent years traveling in the Far East.

- Longfellow refused to allow his son to enlist but reconciled with him after he did so.

- The poem was first published in *Our Young Folks* magazine.

To the Gift Giver

How small is our view of the world, Lord, how limited our understanding of Your work. We expect the world to go according to our plan and rail against You when it doesn't. Then we hang our heads when we are given a glimpse of how wonderfully the greater plan is unfolding. Help us remember that all things work for the good of those who love You—and it's all under your control!

❄

From the Gift Giver

We are troubled on every side, yet not distressed; we are perplexed, but not in despair; Persecuted, but not forsaken; cast down, but not destroyed.

2 CORINTHIANS 4:8–9

Other Wonderful Thoughts. . .

*Nothing that I can do will change the structure
of the universe. But maybe, by raising my
voice I can help the greatest of all causes—
goodwill among men and peace on earth.*

ALBERT EINSTEIN, PHYSICIST AND NOBEL PRIZE
WINNER (1879–1955)

*But peace does not rest in the charters and covenants
alone. It lies in the hearts and minds of all people.*

JOHN FITZGERALD KENNEDY, THIRTY-FIFTH
PRESIDENT OF THE UNITED STATES (1917–1963)

*Common folk, not statesmen, nor generals nor great
men of affairs, but just simple plain men and women
. . .can do something to build a better, peaceful
world. The future hope of peace lies with
such personal sacrificial service.*

HENRY CADBURY, NOBEL PRIZE WINNER
(1883–1974)

*Peace hath higher tests of manhood
Than battle ever knew.*

JOHN GREENLEAF WHITTIER,
POET AND ABOLITIONIST (1807–1892)

13.
Babes in Toyland

The operetta *Babes in Toyland*, just like life and all good fairy stories, contains both good and evil.

Two orphans, Alan and Jane, are sent to their wicked Uncle Barnaby who plans to cheat them out of their inheritance. He arranges for the children to be "lost at sea," while he tries to marry Alan's sweetheart, Mary.

Unhappy with that prospect, Mary—also known as Mary, Mary, quite contrary—runs away to Toyland with her brother Tom-Tom. They seek sanctuary with a toymaker. Unfortunately, the evil toymaker is in league with Uncle Barnaby!

Alan and Jane arrive in Toyland and find the toymaker causing havoc. When the toymaker is killed by one of his own wicked toys, Uncle Barnaby blames Alan. He is sentenced to death, and the only way he can be saved is if Mary marries Barnaby.

In the end Uncle Barnaby proves to be his own undoing, and Alan and Mary are free to marry and live happily after.

Like most classic stories it reflects the grander reality of our existence. Even those of us with mothers and fathers can be seen as orphans in a strange world. This isn't our real home and, at times, it seems to be run by a version of Uncle Barnaby who hates us and wants to steal our inheritance. Our inheritance is, of course, heaven.

Babes in Toyland has a happy ending, and so does our story. Minions of the wicked one will be undone by their own work, just like the evil toymaker. The wicked one, who thinks he is in control, has failure in his very nature.

Mary sacrifices herself to save Alan—but they are both saved and reunited by her sacrifice. Does that remind you of another Babe? Perhaps at Christmastime? One who would go on to sacrifice Himself in love, so that the whole world might have a real happy ever after!

Those Little Extras

- The producers of the operetta were inspired by the stage production of *The Wizard of Oz*.

- *Babes in Toyland* was first produced on stage in 1903.

- Glen McDonough, the writer of *Babes in Toyland*, also worked on *The Wizard of Oz*.

- The story, with a somewhat different plot, was filmed in 1934 and 1961.

To the Gift Giver

Lord, this is a strange world at times, and there are forces at work we cannot possibly understand. For all our conceit of ourselves, we are, if we but knew it, like babes lost in strange land. We don't understand the least part of it all, but we know the one important thing—that you are our Father, and You are walking beside us, holding our hand.

❄

From the Gift Giver

Even so it is not the will of your Father which is in heaven, that one of these little ones should perish.

MATTHEW 18:14

Other *Wonderful* Thoughts. . .

Only those who look with the eyes of children can lose themselves in the object of their wonder.

EBERHARD ARNOLD, FOUNDER OF THE BRUDERHOF
COMMUNITY (1883–1935)

*Children are the hands by which
we take hold of Heaven.*

HENRY WARD BEECHER, CLERGYMAN
AND SOCIAL REFORMER (1813–1887)

*No one has yet fully realized the wealth of sympathy,
kindness, and generosity hidden in the soul of a child.*

EMMA GOLDMAN, RUSSIAN-BORN
POLITICAL ACTIVIST (1869–1940)

*If I could relive my life, I would devote my entire
ministry to reaching children for God!*

DWIGHT L. MOODY, EVANGELIST (1837–1899)

14.
The Nutcracker

Ernst Hoffman was an important nineteenth-century author. Tchaikovsky was. . .Tchaikovsky! Take a story from the former, music from the latter, add the best musicians and dancers in the world, and you have a ballet that still delights audiences more than a century after it was created.

Clara and Franz are lucky children. For Christmas they get exotic dolls that really dance—and a wooden nutcracker! The nutcracker, shaped like a little soldier, is described as a gift for everyone, but when the dolls are put away and the wooden implement is all that's left, Franz is not impressed. He deliberately breaks it!

Clara uses a ribbon from her dress to try to repair him. Sneaking from her room in the middle of the night, she finds the nutcracker leading an army of gingerbread soldiers against the Mouse King's hordes. Weaker because of his break, the nutcracker is almost overpowered by the Mouse King. Clara throws her slipper at the rascally rodent and saves the day.

The nutcracker transforms into a prince and takes Clara to his kingdom, where the Sugar Plum Fairy has been taking care of things. The flowers and the snowflakes dance for her, treats from around the world are presented to her. And, of course, they are wed!

A prince in disguise, come to our world as a gift for us all; a wonderful kingdom that encompasses the world; a battle against evil in which the weak are saved by love; a marriage between our world and a higher one; surely those are themes that deserve to be expressed by our very best artistic efforts.

Meanwhile those of us who aren't artistic, who can't dance or play beautiful music, can applaud. And the next time we see someone down on their luck, we might recall the nutcracker and remember that our Prince often appears among the broken.

Those Little Extras

- *The Nutcracker* premiered in St. Petersburg on 1892.

- It wasn't well received at first, but Tchaikovsky's music ensured it would be given another chance.

- The ballet was first performed in the United States in 1944.

- Since the 1960s this ballet has been a firm Christmas favorite.

To the Gift Giver

We might live the best life we can, but we wouldn't have to look far to find someone who disapproves of some aspect of it. They would be just as sincere in their disapproval as we might be about others. There is no human standard by which all things can be measured, so we need a higher standard. Lord, if we must judge, let it be by Your standard and through eyes of love.

❄

From the Gift Giver

I can of mine own self do nothing: as I hear, I judge: and my judgment is just; because I seek not mine own will, but the will of the Father which hath sent me.

JOHN 5:30

Other Wonderful Thoughts. . .

Outside show is a poor substitute for inner worth.

AESOP, GREEK STORYTELLER (620–564 BC)

Think not I am what I appear.

LORD BYRON, ENGLISH POET (1788–1824)

Things are not always what they seem:
the first appearance deceives many: the intelligence
of a few perceives what has been carefully hidden.

PHAEDRUS, ROMAN STORYTELLER
(C. 15 BC–AD 50)

Be not deceived with the first appearance of things,
for show is not substance.

ENGLISH PROVERB

15.
"White Christmas"

The essence of the song "White Christmas" lies in the first two words of the popular version, "I'm dreaming."

When the song was released, America was at war. Young men on active duty dreamed of home. Those at home dreamed of having them back. Irving Berlin was in California when he wrote it and, according to the omitted first verse, he was dreaming of being "up north."

"White Christmas" is probably the bestselling recording of all time. No one knows how many copies have been sold. It's difficult enough to count the artists who have recorded it!

And what makes it so successful? "I'm dreaming."

What dreams are we reminded of when we hear it? There's the dream of peace. In times gone by, when it snowed everything ground to a halt.

No enemies attacked, little work could be done, people stayed at home, keeping warm with their families.

There's the dream of being loved. The singer sends wishes of "merry and bright" days with every Christmas card they write. How comforting it would be to know that someone was thinking of each of us and loving us.

Then there is the dream of childhood, a time when, in a perfect world, we could lose ourselves in excitement, protected from the harshness of the world by loving parents.

So it's all about dreams.

But the reality of Christmas is that those dreams can be a reality. If we believe, there is God's promise of peace on earth or, at the very least, peace in our hearts. If we believe, there is One above who has nothing but the best in mind for each of us— eternally. If we believe, we can be children again, children of our Father in heaven.

Because of Christmas—even though there was no snow on the first one—the dreams of a white Christmas can become a reality. If we believe!

Those Little Extras

- No one knows for sure, but it is estimated that "White Christmas" has sold more than 50 million copies.

- The song was one of many Irving Berlin hits.

- Berlin himself declared it the best song anyone had ever written.

- Bing Crosby performed it publically for the first time on Christmas Day, 1941.

To the Gift Giver

Lord, it's all possible. Of course it is. You could do it by Yourself, but what would that profit us? Heaven on earth would not be in the magical transformation of this world into a paradise; it will grow from the seeds planted each time we step beyond ourselves to do Your will. Give us the courage to plant a plentiful crop in Your name!

❊

From the Gift Giver

I in them, and thou in me, that they may be made perfect in one; and that the world may know that thou hast sent me, and hast loved them, as thou hast loved me.

JOHN 17:23

Other *Wonderful Thoughts*. . .

Live your beliefs and you can turn the world around.

HENRY DAVID THOREAU,
ESSAYIST AND POET (1817–1962)

Seek not to understand that you may believe,
but believe that you may understand.

AUGUSTINE OF HIPPO, ROMAN BISHOP (394–430)

Some things have to be believed to be seen.

RALPH HODGSON, ENGLISH POET (1871–1962)

Memory believes before knowing remembers.

WILLIAM FAULKNER, WRITER AND NOBEL PRIZE
WINNER (1897–1962)

16.
"The Little Drummer Boy"

Imagine Julie Andrews running across the Alps singing, "The hills are alive, with the sound of. . . drumming"? Well, not quite! But the Von Trapp Family Singers, whose lives were depicted in *The Sound of Music*, did record "The Little Drummer Boy" in 1955!

In the movie, Maria (Julie Andrews) makes a difference to the lives of a wealthy family through simple things, always giving the best of herself. She makes the baron's children play clothes out of curtains, she allows them to climb trees, she lets them snuggle in with her during a thunderstorm. None of these things cost money, but they mean a great deal to the children.

In this song the Magi give their symbolic and very expensive gifts to the baby Jesus; then they call a little boy forward. Being poor, he must have looked at these gifts and been tempted to despair.

He had nothing that could possibly compare. All he had was his drum, probably a toy the likes of which children have played with across the centuries.

So he offered the baby a tune!

Mary nods acceptance and the boy starts playing. It must have been a good tune, because the animals in the stable keep time with it.

What was the result of such an impromptu and seemingly inappropriate gift? Jesus smiles! Why? Because the boy had offered his best to the Lord.

Very few will be able to give as the Magi gave, but each of us can give as the little drummer boy did. He gave a tune. We might give a prayer, a song, an encouraging word, or a helping hand. If we give it to Him (or one of His children) with all our hearts, then it will be enough.

And if Jesus smiles as a result of our efforts, well, could there be a better gift, at any time of the year?

Those Little Extras

- "The Little Drummer Boy" was written by Katherine Kennicott Davis in 1941.

- The song was originally called "Carol of the Drum."

- Rankin/Bass produced a TV special of the song in 1968.

- Romeo Muller, who wrote the TV special of *Rudolph the Red-Nosed Reindeer*, also wrote this television adaptation.

To the Gift Giver

Whether we care to admit or not, Lord, Your law is written in our hearts. While we are subject to and keep "Caesar's" laws we all too often neglect Yours. And, of course, Yours are the most important ones! Magnify them in our hearts, Lord, until they become like breathing and we become wholly honorable and wholly yours.

❋

From the Gift Giver

The Lord is well pleased for his righteousness' sake; he will magnify the law, and make it honourable.

ISAIAH 42:21

Other Wonderful Thoughts. . .

We can do no great things;
only small things with great love.

MOTHER TERESA, FOUNDER OF THE ORDER OF
THE MISSIONARIES OF CHARITY (1910–1997)

I am beginning to learn that it is the sweet, simple
things of life which are the real ones after all.

LAURA INGALLS WILDER, AUTHOR OF THE LITTLE
HOUSE ON THE PRAIRIE BOOKS (1867–1957)

It has long been an axiom of mine that the little things
are infinitely the most important.

SIR ARTHUR CONAN DOYLE, SCOTTISH WRITER,
CREATOR OF SHERLOCK HOLMES (1859–1930)

I rest in Thee, whate'er betide;
Thy gracious smile is my reward.

FREDERICK W. FABER, CLERGYMAN AND HYMN
WRITER (1814–1863)

17.
"Go, Tell It on the Mountain"

"Go Tell It on the Mountain" is a Christmas song—and it isn't!

One of many stirring songs passed down to us from anonymous slaves on the cotton plantations, "Go Tell It on the Mountain" has a rhythm that would make it an ideal accompaniment to the repetitive work of planting and harvesting. One voice would raise it up, others would join in, and the working day would be lifted to a higher spiritual level.

In a way these songs were an expression of the singers' freedom. Every aspect of their day-to-day lives might be owned and dictated by others, but these songs told their "masters" that, ultimately, freedom and love were theirs.

Of course, the song is all about the birth of Jesus. The shepherds, the angels, the manger, and the baby Jesus are all there. So, is it a little disrespectful to call it a working song?

Not at all.

You see Jesus came here for a purpose. His work began on that first Christmas morn, and our part in it begins when we accept Him into our hearts.

What was His work? Why nothing less than the freedom those slaves dreamed about as they sang—freedom in our Lord!

And our work? It's the same as His, in our own little way. It's to bring the salvation of Jesus Christ to our brothers and sisters on earth, to ensure that the whole world knows freedom.

What's the best way to do that? It's our daily dealings with each other, in the way we live our lives, in making sure no child of our Father feels oppressed.

But, if we wanted to spread the Word a bit farther afield—and if we had a loud enough voice— we could always "Go Tell It on the Mountain"! A message like that deserves to be sung "over the hills and everywhere."

Those Little Extras

- "Go Tell It on the Mountain" was collected or written by John Wesley Work, Jr., in 1865.

- Peter, Paul, and Mary recorded a version of the song in 1963 as a civil rights protest.

- John Wesley Work, Jr., was a choral director, educator, and songwriter.

- "Go Tell It on the Mountain" first appeared in print in the 1907 collection *Folk Songs of the American Negro.*

To the Gift Giver

Even at work, even in times of hardship, even in our despair, Lord, we could not help but sing if we truly understood Your works. Because we know that to be true, encourage us to sing Your praises, even when we feel least like doing so. Because, when we get to heaven, we might look back and wonder why we weren't always singing!

❄

From the Gift Giver

What is it then? I will pray with the spirit, and I will pray with the understanding also: I will sing with the spirit, and I will sing with the understanding also.

1 CORINTHIANS 14:15

Other Wonderful Thoughts. . .

When your heart is full of Christ you want to sing.

CHARLES SPURGEON, ENGLISH PREACHER
(1834–1892)

All our life is a celebration for us. . .We sing while we work; we sing hymns while we sail; we pray while we carry out all life's other preoccupations.

CLEMENT OF ALEXANDRIA, BISHOP (C. 150–C. 215)

In almost everything that touches our everyday life on earth, God is pleased when we're pleased. He wills that we be as free as birds to soar and sing our maker's praise without anxiety.

A. W. TOZER, PREACHER AND EDITOR (1897–1963)

God respects me when I work, but He loves me when I sing.

RABINDRANATH TAGORE, INDIAN POET
AND NOBEL PRIZE WINNER (1861–1941)

18.
"Bring a Torch, Jeanette, Isabella"

So, who were Jeanette and Isabella? No one knows, so we have to guess from clues in the song. Someone, perhaps the innkeeper's wife, has risen early and is setting about the morning's chores. Can you imagine the shock when she goes to the stable, as she has so many times before, and finds a baby there?

It's not just any baby. The innkeeper's wife knows straight away that this is the Savior, and she sends Jeanette and Isabella (either her daughters or her servants) to bring lights and to summon all the people of the village! The innkeeper's wife knows this is a major event and important to everyone.

It isn't mentioned, but the poor innkeeper must have got quite a telling off afterward for not providing a comfortable room for this particular expectant mother.

The villagers come running. Some verses talk

of them gathering around the manger in reverential silence, watching the Christ child sleep, commenting on his smile and his rosy cheeks. In other verses the villagers come noisily knocking on the door, holding platters of food, all ready for a celebration. And, indeed, the song was originally a tune for French noble folk to dance a lively jig to at grand meals and balls.

Doesn't that just sum up the feeling of coming to know Christ? On the one hand you want to fall to your knees in supplication. On the other hand, you want to tell everyone about it and start a worldwide party!

Over thirty years later, in the midst of his ministry, Jesus would describe Himself as "the light of the world." At the very beginning of His story, according to this well-loved Christmas song, Jeanette and Isabella helped spread that light with their torches and their enthusiasm for telling people about Him. Now, more than two thousand years later, it's our turn!

Those Little Extras

- The 1553 carol was originally called *Un flambeau, Jeannette, Isabelle*.

- It first appeared in Provence, France, and was not thought of specifically as a Christmas song.

- It was translated into English in the eighteenth century by E. Cuthbert Nunn.

- The upbeat tune was intended for dancing to at parties.

To the Gift Giver

Lord, how can we expect others to see You as their Redeemer if we live lives where You hardly seem to feature? If we grumble about going to church and attend but wish we were elsewhere, why would anyone else come along? Light a fire in us, like Jeanette and Isabella's torches, so others will come to see what (or who) it is that makes the difference in us!

✳

From the Gift Giver

And the next sabbath day came almost the whole city together to hear the word of God.

ACTS 13:44

Other Wonderful Thoughts...

God became man to turn creatures into sons:
not simply to produce better men of the old
kind but to produce a new kind of man.

C. S. LEWIS, ACADEMIC AND NOVELIST (1898–1963)

The birth of the baby Jesus stands as the most
significant event in all history, because it has
meant the pouring into a sick world of the healing
medicine of love which has transformed all manner
of hearts for almost two thousand years.

GEORGE MATTHEW ADAMS, NEWSPAPER COLUMNIST
(1878–1962)

We must not measure greatness from the mansion
down, but from the manger up.

JESSE JACKSON, CLERGYMAN AND
CIVIL RIGHTS ACTIVIST (BORN 1941)

A baby, a manger, a bright and shining star;
A shepherd, an angel, three kings from afar;
A Savior, a promise from heaven above—
The story of Christmas is filled with God's love.

AUTHOR UNKNOWN

19.
"Winter Wonderland"

"Winter Wonderland" is a surprisingly simple but very catchy song. No surprise then that it has been recorded by more than 150 different artists!

Richard B. Smith was thirty-three and recently married when he wrote it, but tuberculosis saw him confined to a sanatorium. It might have been a bleak winter indeed! The frost on the trees and the snow on the hills might have seemed a good deal less romantic—if his wife, Jean, hadn't been working there as a nurse!

No doubt she brought the promise of spring to a Pennsylvania winter. Perhaps some of his recuperation involved walks with Jean in the lane where "snow is glistening" and, in the flush of love, he might well have thought they were "walking in a winter wonderland."

The couple in the song build a snowman and

pretend he is a parson. Wishful thinking? In years gone by parsons, or ministers, would travel a circuit of towns with no regular clergy of their own. Weddings and the like had to wait until his arrival. So these lovers would have been only too keen for Parson Brown to get to town!

Once the job had been done, the newlyweds, much like Richard and Jean, would "dream by the fire" and "face unafraid the plans that we've made."

"Gone away is the bluebird," the lyric tells us. Then it adds, "Here to stay is a new bird. He sings a love song, as we go along."

So who is this new bird who sings love to us as we walk through our lives? Well, He's not mentioned in the song, so I won't shoehorn Him into it. I'll leave it to you to decide if the One referred to in the Book of Psalms as "a new song" is singing love to you as you walk through the wonderland of your life!

Those Little Extras

- Winter Wonderland has been recorded by more than 150 artists, including Doris Day, Frank Sinatra, Elvis Presley, Ella Fitzgerald, Miley Cyrus, Randy Travis, Wynonna Judd, and Cindi Lauper.

- Christmas is never mentioned in the song.

- The often-used verse about the snowman being a circus clown was a later addition.

- Richard B. Smith died the year after the song was published.

To the Gift Giver

What earthly lover ever cared for us and provided for us as You have, Lord? The whole world is a serenade to us, and we usually aren't listening— but You sing on because You truly love us. In return, at church, we sing hesitantly in our hearts. Teach us, O Great Musician, to sing the song of our lives, a song or response from beloved to lover.

❄

From the Gift Giver

And, lo, thou art unto them as a very lovely song of one that hath a pleasant voice, and can play well on an instrument: for they hear thy words, but they do them not.

EZEKIEL 33:32

Other Wonderful Thoughts. . .

Winter is the time for comfort, for good food and warmth, for the touch of a friendly hand and for a talk beside the fire: it is the time for home.

EDITH SITWELL, ENGLISH POET
AND CRITIC (1887–1964)

I wonder if the snow loves the trees and fields, that it kisses them so gently? And then it covers them up snug, you know, with a white quilt; and perhaps it says "Go to sleep, darlings, till the summer comes again."

LEWIS CARROLL (CHARLES DODGSON), AUTHOR
OF *ALICE IN WONDERLAND* (1832–1898)

If winter comes, can spring be far behind?

PERCY BYSSHE SHELLEY, ENGLISH ROMANTIC POET
(1792–1822)

Surely everyone is aware of the divine pleasures which attend a wintry fireside; candles at four o'clock, warm hearthrugs, tea, a fair tea-maker, shutters closed, curtains flowing in ample draperies to the floor, whilst the wind and rain are raging audibly without.

THOMAS DE QUINCEY, ENGLISH ESSAYIST
(1785–1859)

20.
The Littlest Angel

Michael is an eight-year-old boy. A shepherd, living near Bethlehem, he thinks the world is just
full of treasure and excitement. Under his bed is
a wooden box, and in it are some of his most precious things—white stones, blue eggshells, a broken dog collar.

Then, in pursuit of a white dove, he dies and
goes to heaven. His training to be an angel begins,
but it all goes wrong. Michael is still too attached to
his earthly life, his mother, his father, and his box.

Conceding that heaven wouldn't be heaven
without the things that bring us delight, Michael's
guardian angel allows him to fetch his box.

Michael arrives back, just in time for the birth
of Jesus. All the angels are busy fashioning wonderful gifts for Him: a vision never before beheld,
a color never before seen, and music never before
heard.

Michael is stumped. He doesn't have anything to compare, just a box full of stuff he affectionately calls "the treasures of the earth." But he loves it too much to give away!

Then comes a moment. You know. . . that moment when you realize what is right and you content yourself to do it. That's the moment Michael becomes an angel, the Littlest Angel.

He hides his box behind grander gifts, but God knows it is there, and God knows how much it means to him.

The gift that meant more to Michael than anything is raised into the sky. It shines above the earth, and shepherds see it as the Star of Bethlehem, signifying the arrival of the gift that God loved.

There comes a moment when we lay aside our own desires and willingly align ourselves with God's will, our love with His love. That's the moment when God surely smiles, and we become the closest thing possible to an angel on earth—no matter what size we are!

Those Little Extras

- *The Littlest Angel* was written as a radio script. It didn't get produced.

- Hallmark Hall of Fame produced a musical TV special of the story in 1969.

- Fred Gwynne, Herman from *The Munsters,* played Michael's guardian angel in the Hall of Fame production.

- Loretta Young made a recording of *The Littlest Angel* for Decca Records.

To the Gift Giver

What expensive purchase could compare with life? How far would you have to stretch a credit card to purchase pure love? Lord, we know the gifts worth having are from You, and there is nothing we can do in return—except share those gifts with Your other children!

Will You smile then, like a Father who sees His kids turning out all right?

❄

From the Gift Giver

As every man hath received the gift,
even so minister the same one to another,
as good stewards of the manifold grace of God.

1 PETER 4:10

Other Wonderful Thoughts...

If, instead of a gem, or even a flower, we should cast the gift of a loving thought into the heart of a friend, that would be giving as the angels give.

GEORGE MACDONALD, SCOTTISH CLERGYMAN
AND AUTHOR (1824–1905)

Everybody can be great because anybody can serve.

MARTIN LUTHER KING, JR., CLERGYMAN
AND CIVIL RIGHTS LEADER (1929–1968)

*There are souls in this world who have
the gift of finding joy everywhere,
and leaving it behind them when they go.*

FREDERICK WILLIAM FABER, ENGLISH
THEOLOGIAN AND HYMN WRITER (1814–1863)

*It is not the shilling I give
you that counts, but the warmth that
it carries with it from my hand.*

MIGUEL DE UNAMUNO, SPANISH PLAYWRIGHT
AND PHILOSOPHER (1864–1936)

21.
The Amos 'n' Andy Christmas Show

The 1952 *Amos 'n' Andy Christmas Show* came as close to encapsulating the two sides of Christmas as any show could.

First we have Andy, broke as usual, but wanting to do something special for his god-daughter, Arbadella. She has her heart set on a talking doll from the department store. There's no way Andy could afford such an expensive gift, so he signs on with the store as Santa's helper. All afternoon he listens to children, both the naughty and the nice, telling him what they want for Christmas, and he hands out gifts from the store.

His payment for this labor is, of course, the talking doll.

Not wanting to take the credit, he asks Arbadella's daddy (Amos) to be sure and tell her it's from Santa Claus.

Andy leaves and the second part of the story

begins. Amos goes into Arbadella's room to say good night. She asks if she can have the radio on for a little while. He says okay and they listen to the Lord's Prayer being sung over the radio waves. Arbadella wishes they had some Christmas music, and Amos assures her the prayer is the very best Christmas music anyone could have. Line by line, Amos takes the prayer his daughter knows so well and tells her what it means to him.

His retelling of the Lord's Prayer was first broadcast as part of the *Amos 'n' Andy* radio show in 1941. But the prayer which Jesus taught can surely never be told too many times. And we could do worse, each time we say it, to think on just how it applies to our lives.

Separately, but together, the two friends demonstrate the two sides of Christmas: the giving of gifts from the heart and a fresh appreciation of the gifts God gives to us every day. Put them together, and we surely have the perfect Christmas!

Those Little Extras

- *The Amos 'n' Andy Show* ran as a nightly radio serial between 1928 and 1943. Thereafter it developed into a sitcom.

- *Amos 'n' Andy* made it to the silver screen in an RKO-produced movie, *Check and Double-Check,* in 1930.

- When the program transferred to television, the main roles, previously played by Freeman Gosden and Charles Correll, were taken on by Alvin Childress and Spencer Williams.

- In 1988 *The Amos 'n' Andy Show* was inducted into the Radio Hall of Fame.

To the Gift Giver

Prayer is a confusing thing, Lord. Different people have different ways and different routines. Lord, help us make sure our prayer, in whatever form we send it, never becomes routine. And thank You for the perfect example, which we might do well to think about and apply, line by line, to our lives as we say it.

❄

From the Gift Giver

And it came to pass, that, as he was praying in a certain place, when he ceased, one of his disciples said unto him, Lord, teach us to pray, as John also taught his disciples.

LUKE 11:1

Other Wonderful Thoughts. . .

Forgive me my nonsense as I also forgive the nonsense of those who think they talk sense.

ROBERT FROST, AMERICAN POET (1874–1963)

If the only prayer you ever say in your entire life is thank you, it will be enough.

MEISTER ECKHART, GERMAN THEOLOGIAN AND PHILOSOPHER (C.1260–C.1327)

I have been driven many times upon my knees by the overwhelming conviction that I had no where else to go.

ABRAHAM LINCOLN, SIXTEENTH PRESIDENT OF THE UNITED STATES (1809–1865)

In prayer it is better to have a heart without words than words without a heart.

JOHN BUNYAN, ENGLISH PREACHER AND WRITER (1628–1688)

22.

Christmas in Space

Given the chance to tell a story to the whole world, many would struggle to think of anything profound enough. The crew of the Apollo 8 spacecraft might have told about their mission and sung the praises of the engineers who kept them safe and the pilots who had gone before them. Those would have been good stories.

Instead, they chose a better one. With a worldwide audience in the multiple millions, Frank Borman, Jim Lovell, and William Anders read the Creation story from the Bible and signed off with a blessing to "all of you on the good Earth."

The occasion was Christmas Eve, 1968, and a reading about the birth of Jesus might have been more appropriate, but the astronauts were looking at the earth as only God had seen it up to that point.

Sadly, they were seeing a world struggling

with division. America was at war in Vietnam. Martin Luther King, Jr., and Robert Kennedy had been assassinated earlier the same year. And other countries struggled with their own divisions. The astronauts' message was that we were one family, on one world, created by one God.

It's a message that's as valid today as it was back then.

Travelling even further back, to the actual event the Apollo 8 crew were commemorating, we find that God also broadcast a message to the whole world. He didn't use radio waves, He wasn't seen on television. God used a host of angels, and the message they sang was one of hope; hope that was needed then in 1968 and needed no less now. The child in the manger was the answer to all of our divisions.

And the message the angels sang to the world? Simply this: "Glory to God in the highest, and on earth peace, good will toward men."

As a message to the whole world, that's hard to beat!

Those Little Extras

- Apollo 8 was the first manned craft to leave Earth's orbit.

- Borman, Lovell, and Anders became the first humans ever to gaze on the dark side of the moon.

- The journey to the moon took three days, and Apollo 8 circled Earth's satellite ten times in twenty hours.

- Their Christmas message from the moon was, at the time, the most watched TV broadcast ever.

To the Gift Giver

How far have we come, Lord, and how much have we achieved? Yet it serves to show how little we know. We journey to the moon and still miss home, still miss love, still reach out for You. Our greatest achievements, if You're willing, are still to come, and they will be done in the hearts of children, in the bellies of the hungry, in arms wrapped around the unloved. Your work. Right here.

❄

From the Gift Giver

When I consider thy heavens, the work of thy fingers,
the moon and the stars, which thou hast ordained;
What is man, that thou art mindful of him?

PSALM 8:3–4

Other Wonderful Thoughts. . .

The world is so empty if one thinks only of mountains, rivers and cities; but to know someone here and there who thinks and feels with us, and though distant is close to us in spirit—this makes the earth for us an inhabited garden.

JOHANN WOLFGANG VON GOETHE,
GERMAN WRITER AND POLITICIAN (1749–1832)

The world is a book, and those who do not travel read only a page.

AUGUSTINE OF HIPPO, ROMAN BISHOP (354–430)

The most incomprehensible thing about the world is that it is at all comprehensible.

ALBERT EINSTEIN, PHYSICIST AND NOBEL PRIZE
WINNER (1879–1955)

I wanted to write the most beautiful poem but that is impossible; the world has written its own.

DEJAN STOJANOVIC, KOSOVAN POET (BORN 1959)

23.
"Christmas Day in the Morning"

Oh, how we take fathers for granted!

Pearl S. Buck brings it home to us in her short story "Christmas Day in the Morning."

At the age of fifteen, Rob, a farm boy, had no idea his father loved him. It simply hadn't occurred to him either way until he overheard his father telling his mother how much he hated waking him up at four in the morning to milk the cows.

Surprised and touched by this new revelation, Rob decides to give his father the best Christmas present he can. He had already bought him a ten-cent tie, but this calls for something more meaningful. Recalling the Christmas story and the gifts given to the baby Jesus in the stable, he wonders if he might give a gift in their barn (which must surely be similar to a stable).

Early on Christmas morning, Rob puts his natural teenage inclination and his tiredness aside.

He rises well before his father, goes to the barn, milks the cows, and does the other chores. Then he goes back to bed. Shortly afterward his father goes to the barn and find his before-breakfast work all taken care of.

Fifty years later Rob still wakes up early every Christmas morning. He recalls his father's tearful delight and wonders once again at how easy his chores seemed that day when he was doing them for love.

We probably spend more of our lives than we would care to admit taking our heavenly Father for granted. But he loves us all the same, and when we come to realize that. . .well, it's a wonderful thing and we *will* want to thank Him.

What can we do? Well, we can't run the universe, but we can take on some of His smaller chores, like loving one another. And those *will* make a difference to the rest of our lives.

Those Little Extras

- Pearl S. Buck was an American who spent most of her life in China.

- Her Chinese name was *Sai Zhenzhu.*

- Buck was the author of *The Good Earth,* for which she won the Nobel Prize for Literature.

- She won the Pulitzer Prize in 1932.

To the Gift Giver

.Some fathers demand obedience to show that they are the bosses. But good fathers ask things of us that we might grow, that we, in the end, may benefit from them. Because we don't see the long-term aim, we too often rebel. But You, the best Father of all, what can we possibly do for You? And, realizing that, we see that You ask nothing of us for Yourself. It's all for us.

❄

From the Gift Giver

Take my yoke upon you, and learn of me; for I am meek and lowly in heart: and ye shall find rest unto your souls. For my yoke is easy, and my burden is light.

MATTHEW 11:29–30

Other Wonderful Thoughts. . .

When a father gives to his son, both laugh;
when a son gives to his father, both cry.

WILLIAM SHAKESPEARE, ENGLISH PLAYWRIGHT
(1564–1616)

I cannot think of any need in childhood as
strong as the need for a father's protection.

SIGMUND FREUD, AUSTRIAN NEUROLOGIST
(1856–1939)

To gather with God's people in united adoration of the
Father is as necessary to the Christian life as prayer.

MARTIN LUTHER, LEADING FIGURE IN THE
PROTESTANT REFORMATION (1483–1546)

One father is more than a hundred schoolmasters.

GEORGE HERBERT, WELSH POET AND CLERGYMAN
(1593–1633)

24.
Joy to the World

"Joy to the world, the Lord is come! Let earth receive her King."

For people of faith, nothing could be more joyful than the thought of Jesus coming to earth. So the song becomes a firm Christmas favorite and the most-published Christmas hymn in North America.

The fact that it wasn't meant to be a Christmas song should not detract one whit from the joy! Christmas was when Jesus came as a baby boy—albeit a very special baby boy. The time when He will come as King has yet to occur.

English writer and theologian Isaac Watts actually based his hymn on sections of the Psalms referring to the Second Coming. The melody, as we know it now, borrows heavily from another famous piece of musical worship—Handel's *Messiah*! So we have twice the adoration in a single song.

Referring to the time when Jesus would be enthroned as the King of the world, Watts has all of heaven and nature singing His praises. And why not? According to the Gospel of John, everything that was made was made through Him (the Word), so why wouldn't the very hills and the rocks and the trees rejoice at His return?

As for us, what should we do? No doubt we will join in the celebration. But what shall we do until then?

We can delight that the Lord came to earth once. We can eagerly anticipate His second, and final, visit. In between those two happy days we might take a tip from the hymn. In it Isaac Watts urged every heart to "prepare Him room." We should prepare a room in our hearts for the Lord, not a guest room, but a master bedroom, and we can work on making that room a place of joy. Then we can share that joy with the world, just while we're waiting.

Those Little Extras

- "Joy to the World" was published in 1719 in Watts' collection *The Psalms of David: Imitated in the language of the New Testament, and applied to the Christian state and worship.*

- The song has been recorded by many artists, including Andy Williams, Mariah Carey, the Supremes, Dolly Parton, Nat King Cole, and Faith Hill.

- Isaac Watts is often referred to as "the father of English hymnody."

- Being punished by his father for always rhyming, Watts apologized—in rhyme.

To the Gift Giver

Strawberry plants put out runners, which grow into strawberry plants, which put out runners. . . and so on! The joy of the Lord works in much the same way. It's infectious. Joy creates joy, creates joy, creates joy. When we find ourselves in a joyless place, Lord, help us be like a strawberry plant. Help us take the joy You put in our hearts—and put out runners!

❄

From the Gift Giver

His lord said unto him, Well done, good and faithful servant; thou hast been faithful over a few things, I will make thee ruler over many things: enter thou into the joy of thy lord.

MATTHEW 25:23

Other Wonderful Thoughts. . .

I cannot believe that the inscrutable universe turns on an axis of suffering; surely the strange beauty of the world must somewhere rest on pure joy!

LOUISE BOGAN, FOURTH LIBRARY OF CONGRESS POET LAUREATE (1897–1970)

Joy is prayer—Joy is strength—Joy is love— Joy is a net by which you can catch souls.

MOTHER TERESA, FOUNDER OF THE MISSIONARIES OF CHARITY (1910–1997)

There are those who give with joy, and that joy is their reward.

KAHLIL GIBRAN, LEBANESE-AMERICAN POET (1883–1931)

Joy delights in joy!

WILLIAM SHAKESPEARE, ENGLISH PLAYWRIGHT (1564–1616)

25.
The Homecoming:
A Christmas Story

The Waltons are waiting for a miracle in *The Homecoming: A Christmas Story*. The children want to see if the farmyard animals really do kneel to the baby Jesus at Christmas. John-Boy and his mom, Olivia, just want to see John senior safely home again. Working away from home, he has a long, difficult journey to make through the mid-winter snow.

Times are hard on Walton's Mountain, and temptations abound. Ike Godsey tries to convince Olivia that credit at his store is a good thing. The Robin Hood Bandit is stealing from the rich and giving to the poor.

The Baldwin sisters are making moonshine to make ends meet, and a local preacher is working for them. A missionary lady comes to town giving away Christmas gifts, but the Walton children are forbidden to accept charity.

After a heroic effort by John-Boy to find his daddy, John senior makes his own way home in time for Christmas. With him come the answers to everyone's problems and the Walton family say good night to each other in their usual contented and loved manner.

At times we might feel like a family without a father, surrounded by a world of temptation. We might be strong enough to resist. We might give in occasionally. But our Father is coming back, and He is the answer to all our problems, the solution to every temptation.

John Walton brings Olivia a "miracle." Flowers in the dead of winter. A symbol of spring. When she protests that he must have spent all his paycheck on gifts for her and the children, he tells her they will live on love for a while.

If modern times seem to you like a spiritual winter, hold fast to the idea that spring is coming. When Jesus begins His reign, when heaven and earth become one, we will live on love forever. That will be quite a homecoming!

Those Little Extras

- *The Homecoming* aired in 1971. The TV series it piloted ran until 1981.

- Earl Hamner's book, *Spencer's Mountain,* the basis for the series, was based on his own childhood.

- The actors who played Olivia, John senior, and Zebulon (Grandpa) changed between the movie and the series.

- *The Waltons* won an Emmy for Outstanding Drama Series in 1973. Several of its stars won individual awards for their portrayals of Walton family members.

To the Gift Giver

As attached as we might be to this world, Lord—
overly attached at times—there are few of us
who think this is our home. Even the cynical will
sometimes admit to a yearning they can't quite
explain. Thankfully, we realize that this life is but
a journey. There is a home our souls cry out to.
And we will be most welcome when we reach our
journey's end.

❄

From the Gift Giver

In my Father's house are many mansions:
if it were not so, I would have told you.
I go to prepare a place for you.

JOHN 14:2

Other Wonderful Thoughts. . .

*Every traveler has a home of his own, and he learns
to appreciate it the more from his wandering.*

CHARLES DICKENS, ENGLISH NOVELIST
(1812–1870)

*How often have I lain beneath rain on
a strange roof, thinking of home.*

WILLIAM FAULKNER, WRITER AND NOBEL PRIZE
WINNER (1897–1962)

Home is the nicest word there is.

LAURA INGALLS WILDER, AUTHOR OF THE LITTLE
HOUSE ON THE PRAIRIE BOOKS (1867–1957)

There's nothing half so pleasant as coming home again.

MARGARET ELIZABETH SANGSTER, POET, AUTHOR,
EDITOR (1838–1912)

26.
"At Christmas"

"At Christmas man is almost what God sent him here to be." So wrote Edgar Guest (who used to be referred to as the People's Poet) in his poem entitled "At Christmas."

So, what *did* God send us here to be?

We know the story of the Garden of Eden. And then there was the Fall, when the serpent caused Adam and Eve to be banished. Mankind should have been better. We failed. Ever since then we seem to have been at war with ourselves, knowing there is a higher calling but settling for less.

In his poem, Edgar Guest wonders when would be the best time to paint a man. He decides to wait until the man is finished with his selfish battles, has put aside his hate, is no longer sneering or despairing. Some of us are very little different from the man Edgar Guest is contemplating.

He finally decides that the best time to paint a

man would be at Christmas, when "kindness rules him and he puts himself aside." It seems as if at Christmas we are more aware than ever of what we ought to be, and that helps us rise above the spiritual battle that seeks to drag us down at other times.

Famously, in the First World War, the opposing sides in the French trenches declared a Christmas truce. The fighting stopped, the enemy soldiers sang hymns together. They even played soccer among the shell holes.

There are no spiritual truces at Christmas. They aren't needed. That feeling we get isn't a truce. It's a reminder of the power at our disposal; the Power that loves us and will lead us to victory in the end. What we need to do is remember how we are at Christmas, remember what God sent us here to be, then be the same the next day, and the next day, and the next day. . . .

Those Little Extras

- Edgar (Eddie) Guest made his name in America but was born in Birmingham, England.

- His sentimental poems were published and read in the United States for forty years.

- He became Michigan's only ever poet laureate.

- His TV series was called *A Guest in Your Home*.

To the Gift Giver

What is man? Sometimes he is pretty terrible. Sometimes he's amazing. Yet You, Lord, love both. We can be frustrating in our mediocrity— and You love us nonetheless. We can shake our heads, not understanding, or we can try in our small way to be worthy of such care. Made in Your image, we are full of potential. We should reflect a little of that wonder!

❄

From the Gift Giver

What is man, that thou shouldest magnify him? and that thou shouldest set thine heart upon him?

JOB 7:17

Other Wonderful Thoughts. . .

*I do the very best I know how, the very best I can,
and I mean to keep on doing so until the end.*

ABRAHAM LINCOLN, SIXTEENTH PRESIDENT
OF THE UNITED STATES (1809–1865)

*Don't be afraid to give your best to what seemingly are
small jobs. Every time you conquer one it makes you
that much stronger. If you do the little jobs well, the
big ones will tend to take care of themselves.*

DALE CARNEGIE, WRITER AND LECTURER
(1888–1955)

*The best preparation for tomorrow
is doing your best today.*

H. JACKSON BROWN, JR., AUTHOR
(TWENTIETH CENTURY)

Whatever you are, be a good one.

ABRAHAM LINCOLN, SIXTEENTH PRESIDENT
OF THE UNITED STATES (1809–1865)

27.
Miracle on 34th Street

Does Santa Claus really exist? Young Susan, the bosses at Macy's department store, the press, and the American court system all want to know!

Miracle on 34th Street is about whether or not a man calling himself Kris Kringle is actually Santa Claus, but it could also be about the difficulties of faith in a world that demands proof before anything can be deemed real.

As the movie progresses it becomes clear that if Kris Kringle isn't proven to be Santa Claus then an awful lot of people, not the least Susan and the judge trying him, are going to be disappointed. Nobody wants to see him jailed, but everyone, except Susan, feels bound by duty and the requirements of proof.

Once upon a time a skeptic walked out into a wildflower meadow and said, "God, if you're real, give me a sign." Nothing changed. Years later, as a man of faith, he realized that nothing needed to change because absolutely everything he'd seen that day—and every other day—had been a sign. In a way, faith might suffer from an overabundance of proof!

The judge finally accepts Kris Kringle's claim when the United States Post Office acknowledges his reality. The judge and his bench are buried under all the letters addressed to Santa and delivered to Kris Kringle in the courtroom. At that point he can't see anything *but* proof.

Susan gets her perfect Christmas, her mother finds love, and even the judge has a merrier Christmas because of old Kris Kringle.

Of course, that's Hollywood. In real life, if *Miracle* teaches us anything, it shouldn't be that faith is difficult in a world that requires proof; it should be that doubt is amazing in a world where absolutely everything is proof.

God is the "miracle on 34th Street," and every other street, field, mountain, valley, and corner of this wonderful world!

Those Little Extras

- Released in June 1947, the publicity for *Miracle on 34th Street,* made no mention of its Christmas theme.

- The movie won Oscars for Best Actor in a Supporting Role; Best Writing, Original Story; and Best Writing, Screenplay.

- Receiving his Oscar for playing Kris Kringle, Edmund Gwenn said, "Now I know there is a Santa Claus!"

- Childhood star Natalie Wood played Susan.

To the Gift Giver

The world still demands proof, O Lord, but it does so with deceitful intent, aiming to twist words and prove them false. You offer none to them, and I should not be trapped in trying to. Let me offer my life and my works and the courage You will give me as a proof the world can't argue with but might wonder at. And wondering, they might see the Truth.

❄

From the Gift Giver

Now faith is the substance of things hoped for,
the evidence of things not seen.

HEBREWS 11:1

Other Wonderful Thoughts. . .

*Faith is taking the first step even when
you don't see the whole staircase.*

MARTIN LUTHER KING, JR., MINISTER AND
CIVIL RIGHTS ACTIVIST (1929–1968)

*Faith is to believe what you do not see;
the reward of this faith is to see what you believe.*

AUGUSTINE OF HIPPO, ROMAN BISHOP (354–430)

*Faith and prayer are the vitamins of the soul;
man cannot live in health without them.*

MAHALIA JACKSON, GOSPEL SINGER (1911–1972)

Faith is the hand by which my soul touches God.

BILLY SUNDAY, AMERICAN EVANGELIST (1862–1935)

28.
Holiday Inn

The 1942 movie *Holiday Inn* is most famous as the first outing of the Irving Berlin song "White Christmas."

Bing Crosby is Jim Hardy. Tired of the show-biz life, Jim buys a farm and intends to spend his days there relaxing under trees. Of course, farm life isn't quite as relaxing as he imagined it. Still in pursuit of an easy life he turns the farm into an inn—one that only opens for the holidays! Jim insists he isn't lazy; he simply has his own idea of living.

His rendition of "White Christmas" is undoubtedly the most famous scene in the film, but immediately before it is a scene that hardly anyone remembers.

Linda Mason (played by Marjorie Reynolds) is reminiscing with Jim in front of a log fire. She recalls her father as, "Just a man with a family. Never amounted to much. But as long as he was alive we always had plenty to eat and clothes to keep us warm." Jim asks if they were happy and Linda says yes. He draws on his pipe and says, "Then your father was a very successful man."

It's an often overlooked fact that God doesn't ask much of us. Think about all He gives us: life, provision, love, eternity, and trees to sit under. What does He ask in return? That we do what Linda's dad did; that we love each other—and love Him as well.

In this world we often measure success by material gain, disdaining the "little" things. But things like raising a family in love and faith have an effect that echoes down the generations. There's nothing "little" about that kind of success.

Most folk spend the rest of the year trying to achieve the earthly kind of success. Christmas is a holiday from that, when we can connect with God's idea of living—loving each other!

Those Little Extras

- Two of the songs in *Holiday Inn*, "White Christmas" and "Easter Parade," inspired movies of their own.

- As well as writing the songs, Irving Berlin wrote the story of the movie and was nominated for an Oscar for it.

- Fred Astaire costarred as Bing Crosby's best friend/love rival.

- A scene where Crosby is a blackface minstrel and sings about Abraham Lincoln is often cut from screenings.

To the Gift Giver

Lord, Linda's dad never makes an appearance in the movie—but we know he was a good man. Likewise, Your people were supported in their mission by many good souls. People like that are love in action. Help us to care less for fame and reputation and care more for the actual work as You commanded: loving You and each other!

❋

From the Gift Giver

This is my commandment, That ye love one another, as I have loved you.

JOHN 15:12

Other Wonderful Thoughts. . .

Not life, but good life, is to be chiefly valued.

Socrates, Greek philosopher (c. 469–399 BC)

Thank you, dear God, for this good life
and forgive us if we do not love it enough.

Garrison Keillor, author and radio host
(born 1942)

There are two great days in a person's life—
the day we are born and the day we discover why.

William Barclay, Scottish author
and theologian (1907–1978)

People are like stained-glass windows.
They sparkle and shine when the sun is out,
but when the darkness sets in, their true beauty
is revealed only if there is light from within.

Elisabeth Kübler-Ross, Swiss-American
psychiatrist (1926–2004)

29.
"Peace on Earth"
(from Lady and the Tramp)

Anyone who has ever watched Disney's charming 1955 animation *Lady and the Tramp* will remember a studio chorus singing "Bella Notte" over the opening credits. George Givot, the voice of Tony the Italian chef, reprises the song later when Lady and Tramp are falling in love over meatballs and spaghetti.

But how many remember the song that follows immediately afterward? As snow falls around Jim Dear and Darling's house, as jingling sleighs pass by, as the two sweethearts prepare to exchange Christmas gifts, Donald Novis sings "Peace on Earth (Silent Night)," a gentle melody written by Sonny Burke and Peggy Lee. He sings of the Spirit of love and the Child of Peace coming to earth as silently as falling snowflakes, bringing peace and joy to children of goodwill.

Perhaps we shouldn't ignore the lesson in the love story between well-born cocker spaniel Lady and street-wise mutt Tramp. After all, the lesson that love overcomes all barriers and smoothes out all inequalities is an important one.

But that little, often neglected song, "Peace on Earth (Silent Night)," does set the scene for what follows and captures the essence of the season wonderfully. It may even tell us the best way to enjoy our Christmases!

How could it possibly do that, you might ask?

Well, for the clue you need to go to the sheet music. After the song's title and the composers' names, come the instructions on how the music should be played. Those instructions read, "moderately, sweetly with reverence."

We should remember those words as we shop for gifts in crowded stores, as we run out of time, money, and energy! As we get ready for the parties we might stop a while and remember Jesus before all the festivities begin. Then, if we can walk toward Christmas Eve moderately, sweetly, and with reverence, it will truly be a beautiful night, or, as Tony the Italian chef says, a "Bella Notte"!

Those Little Extras

- As well as singing "He's a Tramp" as a dog, Peggy Lee was also the voice of Jim Dear's wife, Darling.

- Larry Roberts, who voiced Tramp, retired from show biz shortly afterward and became involved in the ladies' clothing business.

- George Givot, Tony the Chef, also appeared in *Road to Morocco* and *The Girl Can't Help It*.

- Lee Millar, "Jim Dear," who gives Lady to Darling, also voices the wicked dog-catcher.

To the Gift Giver

It seems so simple, Lord. You don't ask anything complicated. Why do we stray so often? Because there is a battle going on and the enemy uses weapons of mass distraction! Give us the sight and the knowledge to see such things for what they are. Calm our agitated souls so that we might stay with what is real and walk with what is best of all. You, Lord!

❄

From the Gift Giver

He hath shewed thee, O man, what is good; and what doth the Lord require of thee, but to do justly, and to love mercy, and to walk humbly with thy God?

MICAH 6:8

Other Wonderful Thoughts...

The sympathy which is reverent with what it cannot understand is worth its weight in gold.

OSWALD CHAMBERS, SCOTTISH CLERGYMAN, TEACHER, AND WRITER (1874–1917)

Pursue some path, however narrow and crooked, in which you can walk with love and reverence.

HENRY DAVID THOREAU, ESSAYIST, POET (1817–1962)

Man's only true happiness is to live in hope of something to be won by him. Reverence something to be worshipped by him, and love something to be cherished by him, forever.

JOHN RUSKIN, ENGLISH ART CRITIC (1819–1900)

Gratitude bestows reverence, allowing us to encounter everyday epiphanies, those transcendent moments of awe that change forever how we experience life and the world.

JOHN MILTON, ENGLISH POET (1608–1674)

30.
The Wind in the Willows: "Dulce Donum"

Before all the adventures on the riverbank, Mole had a home, but the memory of it had almost left him.

One Christmas Eve he and Rat were battling the elements to get back to the river. Briskly scurrying across fields and carefully making their way through villages, the friends raced against the coming snow.

Then something called to Mole. Perhaps it was scent, perhaps it was instinct, perhaps it was something stronger than either of those. To Mole it spoke of "home."

He suddenly longed to turn aside; to follow that call, but Rat was leading the way. Torn between the longing of his heart and loyalty to a friend, Mole followed Rat. And followed, and followed. . .until he could take it no more. The little mole sat down and wept.

Concerned for his friend, Rat got the whole story and, because he was a friend, insisted they go back and search for Mole's home. Arriving there, he declares it a wonderful home. Carol singers arrive, Rat sends for food, and it all ends well.

We may not think of it in the same terms, but many of us face the same decision Mole wrestled with. We have another home. It is with God. That home calls to those who listen, but we think this world also has a claim to our loyalties. Given the choice between carrying on as usual or introducing a friend to our real home, how often do we choose to go on? How often do we turn aside and follow the call?

Mole enjoyed his riverbank adventures, but on Christmas Eve he realized the importance of an "anchorage" like his old home; a place that would always be glad to see him and would always welcome him back.

The home that's waiting for us is even more wonderful. Maybe this Christmas we can tell a friend about it.

Those Little Extras

- *Wind in the Willows*, by Kenneth Grahame, was published in 1908.

- The success of the book meant Grahame could retire from his post as secretary to the Bank of England.

- The story has been adapted many times for stage, radio, and the screen.

- *Dulce Donum* means "sweetest gift."

To the Gift Giver

Lord, too often we forget what it is to be a son
or daughter of the Almighty. We forget the
homecoming You have in mind for us and how
wonderful it will be. But we also forget that that
inheritance is offered to everyone. This is Paradise
we are talking about. Forever. Give us the
wisdom and the courage to invite our friends—
and our enemies—along.

❆

From the Gift Giver

And Jesus said unto him, Verily I say unto thee,
Today shalt thou be with me in paradise.

LUKE 23:43

Other *W*onderful Thoughts. . .

When I stand before God at the end of my life, I would hope that I would not have a single bit of talent left, and could say, "I used everything you gave me."

ERMA BOMBECK, COLUMNIST AND AUTHOR
(1927–1996)

I have come home at last! This is my real country! I belong here. This is the land I have been looking for all my life, though I never knew it till now.

C. S. LEWIS, ACADEMIC AND NOVELIST (1898–1963)

If you are a Christian, you are not a citizen of this world trying to get to heaven; you are a citizen of heaven making your way through this world.

VANCE HAVNER, CLERGYMAN AND PUBLIC SPEAKER
(1901–1986)

I am still in the land of the dying; I shall be in the land of the living soon.

JOHN NEWTON, CLERGYMAN
AND HYMNIST (1725–1807)

31:
The Gospel Account of Jesus' Birth (Luke 2)

Christmas songs, stories, and movies tend to be variations on one wonderful theme! We get some of that theme from the book of Matthew in the Bible. He's the one who recounts the visit of the Magi, for example, which happened some time after Jesus was born. He tells us of the Immaculate Conception and how Joseph and Mary named their son.

But, for the best description of the night God came into the world as a helpless babe, we need to turn to the book of Luke, chapter 2.

Here we have the busy inn, here we have the manger, here we have the shepherds on the hills, here we have the angels singing, "Glory to God in the highest, and on earth peace, good will toward men." Here we have the recounting that all the other stories, songs, movies, and so on, are based on.

How much trust should we place in Luke's

depiction of the events? Well, he heard about it from eyewitnesses, according to Luke 1:2.

Stories often grow in the retelling. Good stories are retold more than most. A world-changing event like our Savior coming to live among us deserves to be told and told again until the end of time! People, being people, will emphasize some aspects over others; they will interpret things differently; they might embellish the wonders.

Which is why we shouldn't get too caught up in Hollywood's ideas of Christmas, fun as they might be, or the thoughtful interpretations of talented authors, much as they might touch our hearts. Enjoy them, yes. Be uplifted by them, of course. And if they help people to faith, then so much the better. But when it comes to really understanding what happened on that blessed night, spend a little time with your Bible—and read God's version of what Christmas is all about.

Those Little Extras

- As well as being author of the Gospel bearing his name and the book of Acts, some scholars speculate that Luke may have contributed to the book of Hebrews.

- Archeologist Sir William Ramsey described Luke as "a historian of the first rank."

- Tradition has Luke being a painter as well as a physician, and an Indian church claims to possess an icon painted by him.

- The book of Luke is addressed to someone called Theophilus. No one now knows who Theophilus was, but the name means "friend of God."

To the Gift Giver

Father, we sometimes take Your book for granted, and we forget that it came to us through the trials and tribulations of the men and women you chose to convey your message. We give thanks to You today for Luke, Matthew, Mark, and John, who were mere mortals like us. Most of all we thank You for the object of their adoration— Jesus Christ, Emmanuel, God with us.

❄

From the Gift Giver

And it came to pass, as the angels were gone away from them into heaven, the shepherds said one to another, Let us now go even unto Bethlehem, and see this thing which is come to pass, which the Lord hath made known unto us. And they came with haste, and found Mary, and Joseph, and the babe lying in a manger.

LUKE 2:15–16

Other *Wonderful Thoughts*. . .

The perfect Christmas is a myth. After all,
the first Christmas was hardly perfect.
It was glorious and difficult, miraculous and earthy,
sublime and sweaty, tender and harsh.

DAVE MEURER, HUMOR WRITER
(TWENTIETH CENTURY)

To the children, the manger is the chief thought,
to us who are older (though we are all children
together at Christmastime), the Cross always
stands near the manger. It is the background
to every picture, invisible, but there.

AMY CARMICHAEL, MISSIONARY AND WRITER
(1867–1951)

Love came down at Christmas,
Love all lovely, love Divine;
Love was born at Christmas,
Stars and angels gave the sign.

CHRISTINA G. ROSSETTI, ENGLISH POET
(1830–1894)